THE HEART'S JOURNEY

MARIA KITSIOS, LMT

Edited by Jaclyn Reuter
Cover Design by Danijela Mijailovic
Formatting by Maria Kitsios, LMT

ISBN: 978-1-7378369-6-4 (paperback)
ISBN: 978-1-7378369-7-1 (ebook)

Publisher email address: mkitsios8@gmail.com
Printed by Maria Kitsios, in the United States of America.
First printing edition 2022

*Dedicated to all beings
of this incredible world
which I love deeply,
unconditionally,
and eternally.*

INTRODUCTION

The Heart Chakra

According to the Vedas (ancient Indian sacred texts), the physical body is composed of seven main energy or vortex centers called chakras. Chakra is the Sanskrit word for wheel. The seven main chakras run along the spine-beginning from the root and ending with the crown chakra.

1. Root
2. Sacral
3. Solar plexus
4. Heart
5. Throat
6. Third eye
7. Crown

Each chakra has a different color, element, sound, mantra, function, location, major organ, and association. The flow or blockage/imbalance of subtle energy in each chakra determines the health or disease of the individual body.

This book is the fourth of a series of seven poetry books.

It is composed of poems associated with topics of the heart chakra.
The heart chakra is the fourth chakra. It is the one associated with compassion, trust, forgiveness, ability to receive and give love to self and others.

Heart Chakra information:
Sanskrit name: Anahata
Color: Green
Element: Air
Sound: Yam
Mantra: "I Love"
Practice: Gratitude meditation
Function: Compassion, love, healing, connection to self and others, and the bridge between the lower (physical) and higher (spiritual) chakras
Location: Center of the chest
Organ: Heart, pericardium, lungs, diaphragm, arms, shoulders, and ribs
Dysfunctions when imbalanced: Depression, isolation, loathing, holding on to resentment, repressed grief, loneliness, self-centeredness, lack of self-love, high blood pressure, heart attack, asthma, and lung cancer.

1. AS I SPEAK WITH MY HEART

As I speak with my heart,
I tell no lies.
I'm a seeker of Truth
and thus, I will rise!
Growth is uncomfortable—
it hurts, and it pains,
but unless you go through it
only the old you remains.
I find strength
in the here and the Now.
If ever I feel weak,
in prayer I bow.
I trust in the most High
to guide me through,
and I rise from my ashes,
born anew.
As I'm leaving behind
attachments I've held,
I know pain is an indicator
of the depth which I felt.
To move forward
I can't look behind.
It is in uncertainty
my Self I will find.
Healing isn't easy.
You cry and you bleed.
Be kind to yourself
and continue to feed

your heart with light,
love, and positivity.
As I speak with my heart,
I tell it to be patient, courageous and fierce.
Shedding old skin,
conditionings of previous years—
it takes time to change
and evolve in this way.
So, I choose to trust my vision
and guidance today.

2. DEAR HEART

Today and every day,
I am grateful to my heart.
I am grateful its purpose is to keep me alive.
I am grateful for its subtle whispers
which guide me towards the path of Enlightenment.
I am grateful for its simple and humble knowing.

Dear heart,
I apologize if ever I ignored you
or chose a rocky road—
one which tripped you up and bruised you.
I'm sorry.
Please forgive me.
Thank you.
I love you.
I vow to follow your guidance
and live a life in service to you.

3. HEART

Always live from the heart.
Thank your heart
for the endless effort it puts in
to sustain your life
each passing second.
It pumps blood to your body
with such love and grace.
It fills you with compassion
and shares these gifts with the world
every given opportunity.
Your heart has healed
from more bruises
than any other aspect of you.
It has bravely forged ahead
in courageous pursuits.
It has remained open
to love as freely as a child
even in the passing years.
It has tirelessly opened your eyes
to abundance and experience
of the most beautiful kinds.
Your heart has humbly accepted Truth.
Speak kindly to this heart of yours
in awe of its everlasting beauty.
Your heart is braver
than you could have imagined.
For it embodies
the power within.

4. MY HEART IS A MUSCLE

My heart is a muscle
which exercises,
strengthens,
and expands
every time I share my Love.

5. CAPACITY TO LIVE

The heart,
like any muscle in the body,
has torn tissue
from the weight it bears,
but the more weight it holds
the stronger and bigger
the muscle becomes.
So, every hurt
and all the pain you experience
is simply improving
your capacity to live.

6. HEART POETRY

The best poems aren't the ones
written on blank pages.
They're not the ones in ink.
They are the poems written on the heart—
the ones you don't allow anyone to read.

7. OPEN YOUR HEART

A man sits alone by the river,
glancing into its reflection.
The beams seem to embody the waves.
With emptiness inside,
he simply touches the water
and is cooled by its warmth.
Powerful forces are to be found
in all places.
Open your heart.

8. OCEAN OF LOVE

Love is an ocean—
an enormous ocean which overflows,
reaching everything and everyone around it.
Love frees the mind;
it is synonymous with nature.
In the presence of each—
all is One and Holy.

9. OVERFLOW

What is the purpose of having anything
if you cannot share it
or, at the very least,
share your experience of it?
Have you thought about the isolated?
How gloomy their lives must be!
To be unable to offer a smile,
a hug,
or a word to someone else.
Connecting with other beings is connecting with existence, itself.
Each of us is a world of our own—
how phenomenal it is to explore one another's depths
without judgment or ridicule.
When the love in your heart becomes tremendous,
it starts to overflow from the glass of your body.
Then you know you have to share it with others.
This should be understood about Love—
nothing is lost when it is given away.
It is abundant within you and doesn't decrease when shared.
On the contrary,
it grows more powerful and takes over your entire being.
So, love fiercely, love freely,
and be grateful when others accept your offerings of Love.

10. UNITE

Let's all unite
in Love and in Light.
Let's elevate
beyond anger and hate.

Let's all unite.
Let's embrace
this existence
of our human race.

Let's all unite
in Love and in Light.
Let's elevate—
experience peace as we meditate.

Let's all unite.
Let's start to shine—
heal your inner wounds
as I heal mine.

Let's all unite
in Love and in Light.
Release the past,
and remember this life won't last.

II. THE LOVE OF ONE'S SELF

When the love one feels
exceeds one's self,
it has the capacity to fill the world.
When it is powerful within,
it can then multiply and spread to others.
Be the Light which shines within the darkness of time—
the Light which gives man reason to love himself as well,
and thus, the Universe at large.

12. RETURN TO LOVE

Let us return to Love.
Let us return to compassion.
Let us be present with the divinity within.
Let us unite in this sacred place.
All is remembered when we return to this space.
All is possible when we trust and surrender to Divine purpose.
Namaste.

13. LOVE YOURSELF

To have the love of thousands
means nothing
if you don't love yourself.

14. LOVE CREATES

A loving creature is a godly creature—
one which creates.
God is Love and Love creates.
We are the Source we come from—
the place we will return to one day.

15. LOVE IS SIMPLE

Love is simple.
It is acknowledging another person's
body, mind, and presence
as home.
Being able to freely express yourself
with comfort and fearless desire.
It is said,
"A heart which loves is always young."
Keep breathing,
keep loving.

16. LOVE IS A BEING

"When responding to another, think:
If love was a person,
how would he reply?
And then act accordingly."—Al Anderson.
This is one of the most beautiful philosophies
I have ever heard.
Love is a person—
a person who is aware, empathic, and conscious.
Let each of us be this person.
Let us be reminded of our true nature and spread Light
onto an otherwise dim and cruel world!

17. LOVE IS A PERSON

Love is a person,
and that person is you.

18. LOVE IS LONELY

In a guarded and fearful world,
Love is a lonely being.

19. A LONELY PERSON

Being a loving person in this world
means you are a lonely person.
Few understand you,
and even fewer appreciate you.

20. LOVE IS GOD

Be your grandest Self
even if others can't deal with it.

Be the embodiment of the Divine
even if others are so scared
of their love for you
that they unconsciously push you away.

It takes courage to love—
to flow and build
with Love.

It's hard for a guarded person
to be around a loving one.
A lover tears down walls
with his presence alone.

It takes a lot of trust and surrender
to embrace a loving being.

God and Love are often lonely.

21. PILLARS OF LOVE

Compassion and acceptance
are the pillars of Love.
They naturally manifest from within
when you are kind to yourself.
They grow from the awareness
that we are currently in human form—
here to make mistakes and learn.
When you bathe in this awareness,
compassion and acceptance arise easily,
and you guide others with both.
If you have suffered,
you choose to help those who suffer.
You understand that many times
people act from a place of trauma, fear, or pain,
and their actions are not a reflection of their truest nature.
Acceptance helps us see that people go through
the exact experiences they need
in order to grow.
All we can do is be kind to one another
during this fleeting experience we call life.

22. A BYPRODUCT

The greatest disservice is often done
from the concept of opposing forces:
right and wrong.
This idea of duality
feeds the ego and encourages division.
In a Universe full of possibilities and probabilities,
how can any one way of doing things be right?
There is no right or wrong way of life.
Each person simply goes through
personal experience within a collective consciousness.
So, instead of judging others,
listen to learn about their experience.
It will help you grow—
grow in Love.
To be in Love is to embody
compassion and acceptance of the Oneness in all.
Compassion comes easily if you have suffered.
For only the survivors of pain can empathize
with those who are hurting.
Acceptance is a byproduct of compassion.
Accept each individual's particular state of being
without judgement
in any given moment.

23. ACCEPTANCE

Things aren't always the way
we imagined they would be.
Acceptance of what is
is important.

24. ACCEPT IT

Sometimes
you just have to say,
"It is what it is,"
and learn to embrace acceptance.

25. BE TENDER

Compassion—
the only way to alleviate suffering;
the only way to rid of negative,
internal and external turmoil.
One can never be angry or hateful towards another
if one understands and feels for the other.
We are all imperfect human beings,
perfect in our imperfection.
Strive towards growth into the best version of yourselves.
Be tender, be soft, be compassionate.

26. COMPASSION

The softest and most compassionate hearts
are the strongest and wisest of all.

It takes strength to choose compassion
when someone is hurting you,
wisdom to understand their actions stem from trauma,
courage to step away from ego
and embrace the calmness of your Higher Self
in the midst of emotional turmoil.

Although we are not responsible
for eradicating another's trauma
we should avoid adding to it.
When we truly understand
the suffering of another,
we become conscious to not cause more of it.

We might find in such moments of compassion
we are able to trigger healing ability within the other.
It is with these small steps,
we help each other grow.
Darkness doesn't exist when we shine our Light on it.
And ultimately,
we are guiding one another
towards Light.

27. COMPASSION'S HOME

No anger or sadness can exist
where compassion built a home.

28. HIMSELF

God uses each of us to experience Himself.

29. REALM BEYOND

Life always brings us back
to humbleness and humanness.
All we ever have
is what we carry
to the realm beyond.

30. ONE WISH

If I had one wish
it would be
for each person to open up his heart,
laugh a little more,
love a lot more,
and see all the beauty which lays within
in order to bring it to life again.

31. THAT IS LOVE

The ear when you need to vent,
the hug when you are cold,
the caress when you are sore,
the distance when you need to be alone—
that is Love.

32. LOVE OF ALL THINGS

I only wish to have touched
a single soul
as much as beauty touches me
every day.
The beauty of the enormous sky,
tiny stars staring down at us,
warm hugs of caring friends,
memories left behind with passing time,
the very subtle and present changes of nature—
tiny miracles of perfection.
If I am to die tomorrow,
I will be at peace,
for I've lived this life well,
for I know Love of all things.

33. MY NATURE IS LOVE

My nature is Love.
My nature is joy.
My nature is peace.
Never do I feel as satisfied as when
I do something positive for another.
Never do I feel as blissful
as the moment I act selflessly.

34. RISING IN LOVE

In your presence,
I know Love.
Our connection raises me above
all which is Earthly,
and so, I soar the skies
flying through the sun
to the greatest heights.

I'm rising in Love,
never falling for you.
Rising in Love,
being anew.

In your presence,
I know Love
like never before.
Rising above
the eager heart
which yearns for more-
'cause I'm rising in Love,
never falling for you.
The warmth of your hugs
and the playing we do.

I'm rising in Love,
never falling for you.
Rising in Love,
being anew.

In your presence,
I know Love
in the subtlest ways—
no lack thereof.
Our connection is
abundantly blessed—
in lifetimes present, future,
and all of the rest.

I'm rising in Love,
never falling for you.
Rising in Love,
rising in Love with you.

35. ROMANCE

Your presence is my sanctuary.
Your love is necessary.
Your embrace is my peace—
soothing as an autumn breeze.
I thought I knew romance before,
but it's only you I adore.
So, take me in your arms and hold me tight.
Let's travel on this journey and share the ride.

36. THE GARDEN OF MY HEART

When my lips felt yours
it reminded me that I have
waited for your kiss
entire lifetimes now.
It is the perfect texture
and taste.
I could stay here forever—
inside your embrace.
Your moist mouth
waters the garden of my heart.
'cause baby,
making love is an art.
It is here I desire to be.
The only truth I deeply know.
So, I sit back
and watch this love grow.

37. SOFTLY GUIDES

A person who loves you is one who softly guides you back to yourself.

38. GREATEST OATH

Let each moment remind us
to return to Love,
if ever we have strayed away.
Even in moments of anger,
let us remember
to return to Love.
This shall be our greatest oath.
Let us vow to always
return to Love.

39. SWEET HONEY

For all that you are to me—
I thank you, my sweet honey.

40. WINDS REMIND OF LOVE

The wind reminds of Love.
It may soothe us one minute,
chill us the next.
Nevertheless,
it does not cease to touch us.

41. APPRENTICE OF LOVE

Let's be an apprentice of Love
to one another.
Let's learn the best way
to love each other.
Teach me to be patient
and worry less.
I'll teach you to live
in selflessness.
Let's be an apprentice of Love
to one another.
God created us
to love each other.

42. SURRENDER TO LOVE

Never in my life
had I imagined
loving someone so deeply
that whether that person loves me in return
is none of my business.
This is how I know-
I am being guided into complete surrender and trust.
I vow to always honor this love
and stay true to my heart.

43. MY ONE

Slow love is everlasting,
I've been told.
There's magic
in the hands we hold.
I could look at your face
every day 'til I'm old.
A harmonious face
filled with Love and Light.
In this sacred place of connection
we vow to endlessly unite.
Fingertips touching
the center of my palm.
I know this is right for me
because I feel calm.
And my dearest,
you'll always be my one.
Slow love is the way
alchemy is done.

44. IN LOVE WITH ME

Stand still,
present in Love
with me.
Let the silence of us
transcend time
and echo into eternity.
Be present in Love
with me.
Meditate beside me
and fill yourself with my energy.
Be present in Love
with me.
Let the magic of us
manifest effortlessly.
Here, present in Love
with me.

45. LOVE ME IN THE DARK

Love me in the dark—
gently caress my shadow here.
Take this part of me into your embrace—
hold it close and near.
It has been bruised, betrayed,
and battered into fear.

Love me in the dark—
I am not always in the Light.
Let us share words to understand—
I do not need to constantly be right.
If I am heard with compassion,
then I feel alright.

Love me in the dark
and stay regardless.
No one has my heart
when I am at my best.
Sometimes it's my head
which needs the extra rest.

Love me in the dark
or leave me here instead.
Resentment is a part
of all that's left unsaid.
So, let me speak my truth
before you bury me for dead.

Love me in the dark.
If you choose to leave,
go on now ahead.
I've dealt with so much loss,
there's nothing here to fret.

Love me in the dark
or you don't deserve my shine.
If you're not passionate about me
then you're not really mine.
So, if you think it best to leave
I'll accept it and be fine.

Love me in the dark
for we all have a shadow side.
I expose all of the demons
others prefer to hide.
Shine Light into my dark spots,
so they may subside.

Love me in the dark.
I am unique and one of a kind.
You'll always seek out
my spirit, heart, and mind.
A woman like me
you'll never find.

46. LOVE ME

Love isn't a feeling
which takes over your being.
It isn't desire
burning like wild fire.

Love is a building
with strong foundation in place.
It isn't a sprint,
but a marathon race.

It takes time
and nurturing to grow.
Commitment to stay
and the other to know.

When the blocks
are solid and strong,
you realize it is
where you belong.

Then you see the marvelous view
from the mountaintop
and you smile as you whisper
"Love me, love me. Never stop!"

47. GOLDEN HANDS

My hands are golden—
for all the works I have written.
As are my eyes,
for they have glanced upon yours.

48. POET'S LOVE

To be loved by a poet
is to eternally be
engraved in
sweet poetry.

You are remembered
in books and memory.
In union, creation,
and ceremony.

To be loved by a poet
is to be
held in warmth
compassionately.

You are mentioned
in sacred prayer.
Blessed each moment
with Love so rare.

49. UNCONDITIONAL LOVE

Learning to love unconditionally is a painful process.
You slowly shed old patterns
which dictated a huge part of your life.
You battle with your ego constantly
and such an internal battle isn't easy.
You let go of insecurities
and the need to be loved in return.
Your mind tries to talk you out of it
because of the conditioned fear
of being taken advantage of.
We have many unhealthy layers
inflicted upon us by society and upbringing.
But knowing you are Love,
knowing what it means to truly BE Love
overpowers all the human nonsense.
It overpowers the unnecessary jealousies,
the negative voices in your head—
all of it.
For Love is wanting the happiness of another
even if you aren't the one providing that happiness.
We shall all strive to achieve such a loving state,
regardless of how painful the process may be.

50. ALL OF IT

I am going to have
a 'set your body on fire,
calm your mind,
and lighten your spirit'
kind of Love.

All of it.

Embracing
the Holy Trinity of me.
Only that type of Love
is better than solitude.

51. SOUL PARTNERSHIP

I like to believe
we meet each other again
in the next cycle,
where we no longer hold
the same faces or names,
where we change
in form and voice.
I like to believe
we meet each other again,
endlessly
throughout an infinite existence
under the stars and expansive skies.
And yet,
we smile in recognition
every time
because within us, we know.
We travel through dimensions
to reunite in Love again.
A constant chemical reaction
of atoms and molecules
which attract each other
in formless realms.
It is these in-between
moments of separation
which bring unease and pain
for we yearn to be back home—
the home of soul partnership.

52. PRAYER FOR US

In all the edges
of the mind's canvas
I find smooth waves
with the colors of you.
In blends of shape
and swirls of dust,
the image of your smile appears.
I hear the subtle beats
of my heart,
and they whisper your rhythms.
In all the beauties
of wisdom's eye,
I glance upon your presence.
In every emotion I touch,
I palpate your warmth.

In an unknown future,
I know I will carry you
inside of me—
as I have done for lifetimes now.
Yet somehow,
we were able to find each other
in different skin
and new identity.
We are the same
of highest entity.

Soul recognition

brought us here again.
My lover, my guardian,
my eternal friend.
And if for whatever reason
we are to part,
I will come to feel the distance
in my heart—
the soul's yearning for
our reunion once more.

For in the ecstasy
of all the mountaintops,
blissfully
and in peaceful currents of the sea,
I always wish
to have you here with me.
So, I carry you—
knowing in comfort you are here
somewhere amongst the stars
breathing in the air,
envisioning my presence too.
If the worlds come to an end
and realities crash down upon us
you, my love, will always be my friend.
In silence I pray
we're abundantly connected, thus.
This is a prayer for us.

53. A LOVER

I am a lover
who makes love to her thoughts
and thus creates
innovative ways to be an instrument of Light
in each waking moment.

54. MANIFEST A TRUE LOVER

Manifest a true lover,
and don't settle just to settle.
Being alone is better
than being with someone who hurts you.
You deserve a loving life partner—
one who elevates you,
calms your mind,
excites your body,
pushes you to grow,
and nurtures your heart.
You deserve it.
Don't settle for mediocre—
manifest the greatest kind of Love.
Otherwise, why not stay alone?

55. THERE ARE NO HALVES

There are no halves.
No one is here to complete you.
A partnership is about empowering and motivating each other
to reach new heights individually and collectively.
Be whole within yourself to embrace
healthy and loving connections with others!

56. CHOOSE LOVE

To see and know all
and still choose to be Love regardless—
I think that's one of the bravest acts.
No one should be given the power to hurt you
to the point where you stop being Love.

57. EXPOSED

When you give all of your love openly,
exposed and completely vulnerable
and yet, it is rejected,
you start to wonder
if you are worthy.
When your love is not enough to sustain connection,
it's inevitable to start thinking you are not enough.
Don't give anyone the right to make you doubt yourself.
Don't give anyone such power.
No matter how much you love someone,
always love yourself more.
No one is here to define you or complete you.
Define yourself in such a firm way that no one's rejection
can shake your deepest roots of self-love!

58. NOT AGAIN

You'll never see
that me again.

You were the one who killed her—
strangled her to death.
You'll never get to touch her
or feel her heavy breath.

Your hands tossed her aside
and broke her part by part.
Even as her heart gets torn
with every inch you grow apart.

Even if she silently cries
as she severs your bond.
If you pushed her away,
don't be shocked when she's gone.

Even when she yearns
to hold you tight,
I'll continue letting go
with all my might.

Even when she wants
to make her presence known,
I'll remind her
she's better off alone.

And if I ever see you,
I won't look you in the eyes.
For in there you may witness
Love within me still resides.

But like I said before
she was transparent then.
You'll never see
that me again.

59. GOOD FOR ALL

Let Love lead the way.
The mind is good for some things,
but the heart is good for all.

60. WORTH HAVING

The only thing worth having to give away is Love.
The only thing worth holding onto is the Love within.
Everything else escapes and slides away,
especially when you try to hold it tightly.
Whether it be material possessions or other people.
Everything in this world is in a constant state of change
and nothing ever remains the same.
Learn to let go of all
besides that which is in your spirit,
and be free in a world of slavery.

61. WITH EVERY HEARTBEAT

With every heartbeat,
every inhale and exhale,
I find the soul aging.
The body takes different forms
and the face changes on its own.

With every heartbeat,
every inhale and exhale,
I am a new person.
As I learn and grow
in this new moment of awareness.

Each heartbeat is a lesson:
each breath is a lecture and a teaching.
So, when you meet me,
remember me in detail
(as I am that given moment)
for I will never be the same again.

And if we were previously introduced,
I'd like to shake your hand once more.
If our paths ever cross again,
I'll be a stranger then.

With every heartbeat,
every inhale and exhale,
I take on new life.

So, if ever I hurt you
or did you harm
learn to forgive and let go.
You wouldn't recognize me anymore.

62. DIFFERENT PERSON

It pains me to know
some people carry negative experiences
because of something I may have done to hurt them.
However,
I do not hold any anger towards myself
because I did the most I knew at the moment.
I am a different person now.

63. HEAL AND GROW

If ever I did you wrong,
forgive and let it go.
That same person
isn't here anymore.
And if you did something to hurt me,
you'll still never be my foe.
That was you then,
but I don't know you anymore.

Seasons change,
spirits grow,
things are passing
to and fro.

Please forgive me if I ever made you cry
or took away your hope.
That cruel version of me
exists no more.
If you ever did me dirty
I forgive you, so you know.
We each have the right
to heal and grow.

Seasons change,
spirits grow,
Love awakens
in the flow.

We each come to realize
Love is all.
And when we do,
we let go of any thought
which isn't so.

64. LEARN FROM THOSE

You always learn the most
from those who hurt you greatest.

65. EXPERIENCE LEARNS

There is much through innocence
which experience learns.

66. FORGIVENESS PRAYER

Cutting ties
requires us to forgive.
Prayer helps in this need to let go.
This is a forgiveness prayer:
May you find someone whom you can love,
and most of all, may it be yourself.
May you heal your anger and pain
and may it leave your body now.
May my absence contribute to your journey
towards growth and compassion.
May you see the truths
you so ruthlessly defend against.
May you use this opportunity to look at your trauma
with the eyes of honesty.
May you gain the courage to throw it all away.
May your inner speech become kinder, more loving,
so you may speak with others in a warmer way.
May your mind sharpen and your heart soften,
so you understand which path is best for you.

67. EVOLUTION OF THE SPIRIT

Forgiveness is
looking at the person who harmed us,
seeing a human being,
and acknowledging the imperfect state of humanness.
Forgiveness is
understanding that people who are hurting,
hurt other people.
As painful as their offense might've been,
it was done because they were suffering.
Anything which is within us
overflows to the outside world,
thus, affecting those closest to us.
But if we have Love within us,
we bring joy to everyone around us.
All of this makes forgiving easier.
Forgiveness lifts all negativity from our hearts
and we become more compassionate in the process.
We are all here to learn and grow
into our wholeness
and our nature of Love.
It isn't easy handling injustice
with kindness,
but it is necessary
for the evolution of the spirit.

68. I THANK ANYONE

I thank anyone who hurt me.
Now I know to care for myself.
I thank anyone who failed to love me.
Now I know how to love myself.
I thank anyone who couldn't see my worth.
Now I know I am worthy.
I thank anyone who walked out of my life.
Now I know not everyone adds value to it.
I thank anyone who made me cry.
Now I know to appreciate joy and laughter.
I thank anyone who doubted me.
Now I know to trust my intuition.
I thank them all
even though I will never cross paths with them again.
I am different now.
Our frequencies are no longer aligned.
And I know they were just vessels from Source—
teaching me important lessons about my Self and existence.

69. GRATEFUL

I am thankful
for the food
Mother Nature
grows so well,
and for the shelter
which houses my spirit.
I am thankful for all
the people I have met,
the close ones and others
I didn't have the chance
to know so well—
for those I've met
and those I haven't,
but still share this world with.
I am thankful
for everything I lived.
It has made me strong.
I am thankful for the Universe
and for life!

70. GRATEFUL FOR ALL

I am grateful for darkness,
for within deep darkness there is abundant Light.
I am grateful for hardships,
for within hardships there is delicious nectar of growth.
I am grateful for friends and foes alike,
for we can learn necessary lessons from all.
I am grateful for the body,
for its impermanence houses the eternal spirit.
I am grateful for death,
for it shows us the value of a life well lived.
All around us is something to be thankful for
when we see the beauty and possibility in everything.
If only we are willing to open our hearts to see.

71. YET ANOTHER BREATH

This is a reminder—
life only exists in the present moment.

The past and the future are simply fantasy.
The past is a dream long gone,
the future imagined only in the racing mind.

Being fully in the present
creates miracles.
Only in the Now do we ever truly exist.
And Now is the most beautiful place to be.

Be still and feel yourself.
In this moment, you are alive.
Honor this space.
Be grateful for yet another breath.

72. GRATEFUL, BLESSED, THANKFUL

I am grateful, blessed, and thankful!
I am in Love.
This phrase is often misunderstood.
We usually use it to describe our feelings
towards another person.
But have you payed attention
to those words?
I am IN Love.
Meaning I am consumed by Love,
I am in the middle of Love as it surrounds me
and engulfs me.
Love overflows out of me and into all it touches.
This is the real meaning.
It does not need to be directed
towards one specific person.
Love is my nature.
So, I am IN Love.
I will forever be.

73. GRATITUDE ATTITUDE

My attitude is gratitude.

74. LOVE IS PRAISED

Valentine's Day.

On this day where love is praised,
let us remember to praise
the greatest love of all—
Divine Love.

Let us remember to strengthen
our most important relationship of all—
our relationship with the Creator.

Let us remember to take time
and connect with God
through prayer,
nature,
sacred interactions with our fellow beings,
and the wisdom within the physical body.

Let us remember that we are never alone
when we embrace divinity in our lives.
May we celebrate the gift of life
and remain grateful to God
for the Love we encounter every day,
in every breath,
every opportunity to be present
with our Highest Self.

75. DEFINITION OF SELF-LOVE

There are many ways to love myself,
and they change often.
Sometimes it is by pushing myself,
others it is in taking rest.
Therefore,
the best definition of self-love is
in each moment
I choose to act and think
in a way which assists
my spiritual growth.
I choose to act from a place
of higher perspective.
So it is,
so it is,
so it is.
Now and always.

76. STANDARDS

I love myself too much
to stay with someone who hurts me deeply.

77. MY PURPOSE

When I'm at my optimal health—
improving and embracing my Higher Self-
I'm better able to serve and elevate others.

Self-care is a very selfless act.

I have a uniqueness which is my own.
It encompasses my purpose.
I'm only able to share all of me
when I'm present in the state of Love,
in the current moment of awareness,
and radiating at a high frequency.

It is then I can embody my grandest qualities:
Leadership, fearlessness, and compassion.

I'm here to lead by example
and show others the simple truth about themselves:
We are divine and humble beings.
We have purpose here.

My purpose is to remind others
of their spiritual essence
and bring them back to themselves,
back home.

78. SPIRITUAL REALIZATION

If in any moment we knew the other would die,
would we continue being cruel to one another?
If we truly understood how temporary life is
would we continue to lack compassion?
Maybe we would hug the other—
being present in Love.
Maybe we would finally appreciate each other.
Maybe we would be gentle with another's heart.
Maybe we would come to know
the full expression of unguarded devotion—
vulnerable and exposed.
Maybe we would lose count of wrongs
and forgive our imperfect humanness.
Maybe we would have a spiritual realization
for in the face of death
we come to see who we are.
This is how I know
I would die for those I love.
Again and again and again.

79. GIVE HEALING

Elevate your spirit,
open your heart,
and let Love overtake your life.
Embody compassion so other lost and hurt souls
might be a little less lost
and a bit more peaceful after your encounters
in this temporary form we call humanity.
Give healing to the world.

80. GIVE

I find that most people yearn
to be loved,
to be heard,
to be accepted.
It'll surprise you to know
most people don't receive enough
care and kindness
from those close to them.
They are sometimes too consumed
by their own thoughts
to be of service.
Therefore,
I take time
and hold the space
to provide all this to the world.
And by "the world"
I mean everyone
I come into contact with.
As a godly being,
it is my greatest responsibility
to leave others better than I found them.
Even if it is by giving
a simple, loving hug.

81. FULL HEART

When I think of you, my heart is full
and I am then the woman I always want to be.

82. FILL YOUR HEART

Do the things which fill your heart with joy,
your life with laughter,
and your spirit with Light!
Love, my fellow beings.
Love!

83. EMPOWER THE HEART

There's no greater feeling than what you experience
when you do something kind for someone else.
Nothing feels more pleasant.
So, be compassionate
and kind to others
today and always.
Empower the heart chakra.

84. SPECIAL

Not only do you owe it to yourself
to be the best you possible,
not only do you owe it to yourself
to reach your full potential
and self-actualize,
you owe it to every person
you encounter in this lifetime
for there is no one else like you.
You are unique.
You are blessed with being
the only you out there,
in all of the Universe.
And so,
you owe it to existence
to let all your beauty shine,
to touch others
in the way only you were born to do.
Otherwise,
the world will miss out on meeting
the essence of you.
I urge all to heal and grow
because the rest of us are eager to see
the best of each of you!

85. SIMPLICITY

Happiness is simplicity—
a hot tea on a cold night,
a sky filled with stars dancing in synchronistic flow,
a bed to lay on,
and Love in your heart—
my traveling spirit!

86. TRAGEDY AND COMEDY

When we think of lost loved ones,
we shall think of them in gratitude—
gratitude for having met and bonded with their soul.
It is an honor to meet one another.
The memories and stories of their human form are legacies.
They shall make you smile
for those moments reveal love.
They reveal the spirit of a person,
like photographs capture emotion in a given time.
Our life is a movie.
Sometimes a tragedy
and others a comedy,
but it is the chemistry between the actors
which makes it fantastic!

87. HUMOR

A spiritual being is also a funny one.
It's impossible to understand our true nature
without having a sense of humor at the contradictions in it.
When you truly understand,
everything is hilarious because it's so temporary.
You often think to yourself,
"Silly mind!
You're so silly for letting anything affect
this precious, present moment."
Here I go returning to meditation again.
The moments of returning home.

88. LAUGHING

In a world where people take everything
(especially themselves)
so seriously,
I want to be laughing,
loving, and openly free to be me.
And if someone comes along to ask me
why I am so wild,
I'll dance around
and fiercely shout
"Because I trust in Source
to lead my soul
to its greatest desire,
to the strongest fire
that'll burn to ashes
all which no longer serves
my growth."
We are here to heal,
starting with ourselves,
and helping others do the same.

89. PLAYFUL

It is important to embody a playful spirit—
to laugh and dance—
especially during dark times.
It is therapeutic and puts things into a lighter perspective.
The bonus is we are better able to handle any situation
and any negative circumstance
when we choose to remain positive.
It too shall pass as
everything always does.
This does not mean denying
negative emotions which arise within us.
We are human, after all.
Notice the emotions,
but choose to stay in your Light
by laughing and loving still.
Even if others don't understand you,
refuse to get drawn into negativity.
Live your life
in sacred and powerful presence.
It is your masterpiece,
so keep on creating
and stay true to your inner truth!

90. PLAYGROUND OF LIFE

I am a child
who wants someone to play with
on this playground of life.

91. CHILDLIKE STATE

The search and yearning for happiness
is the indirect desire to return to our childlike state.
For a child leads with his heart,
does things out of pure intuition,
and has no fears of the future
because he lives only in the present moment.

Fears arise in the thought of losing something,
but when you hold on to nothing,
you do not fear losing anything.
In all this we see that only a child
knows how to truly love.

92. INNER CHILD

As the years go by
somewhere deep within us,
the inner child is still alive—
the part of us we may
have tried to,
or continue to, silence—
the sensitive, loving,
playful, and selfless little being
which wants to connect.
The inner child
looks vulnerable to us.
We are adults now
so, we think we don't need anyone.
We disguise ourselves
in independence
and hardened shells—
masks woven long ago.
But regardless of the tape we use
to keep his lips closed,
the child continues
to cry out at night—
cries which wake us in the middle
of restless sleep,
asking for our attention and protection.

93. CHILDHOOD EXPERIENCE

Children are the Light of God.
Constant displays of the purest Love
is the childhood experience.
It is a blessing to be in such presence.
We learn so much about who we really are—
abundant Love!

94. CHILDHOOD

It is difficult to be a child.
We always think they have it easy,
but they are constantly given attention
even when they'd prefer to be left alone.
They are constantly being told to listen
because they don't know.

But there are many things they know
on a deeper level than the rest of us.
We must remember they recently came here
from Source.
They haven't been polluted by the world yet
nor has the matrix warped their vision.
Be quiet and listen to them more often.

I think being a child is a very lonely experience.
We are hardly understood or seen in adulthood—
a statement which is amplified in childhood.
Everyone gives them attention,
but doesn't truly see them.

95. HOLD ON, LET GO

Hold on to the beautiful memories
and let the negative go.
But how?
How to hold on to anything
when you're letting go?

96. NEVER HOLD

One day we will need to let go of everything,
including this body.
How quickly it passes us by.
Too much so
that we should never hold
anger or hatred in our hearts.

97. POWERFUL DEVICES

The most breathtaking of moments
are hardly documented photographs.
No devices are powerful enough to capture them
except the heart and mind.

98. HEART BLOCKAGE

A heart which is blocked
doesn't allow blessings to enter it.
Be courageous enough to accept the miracles of life—
miracles which only an open heart allows.
You are worthy and deserve to connect with
the beauty of such experience every moment
of your temporary life.

99. PERICARDIUM

There is a ring
around my heart
which covers the organ.
It tightly wraps itself around it
in protection.
But sometimes,
the grip becomes overwhelming
and squeezes the heart
more than it can bear—
the way a lover
erotically keeps his hand
around my neck
until I begin to suffocate.
I can feel it cutting
my breath short.
This ring has only added
further despair.
Might as well
have never been there.

100. TOO GUARDED

You are too guarded
to truly experience the beauty of us,
so you don't deserve to.

101. GUARDED WORLD

I may hurt more deeply and often than others
by leaving my heart open
in a guarded world,
but I also receive more Love
than is imaginable.

102. OPENLY

I connect more with trees and the sun
than I do with most people.
The trees and the sun want to give and receive
Love and connection openly.
Humans are not this way.
They're wrapped in fears and insecurities.

103. OPENING UP TO YOU

We each have a set of beliefs which guides us
through our daily lives.
We are usually eager to share and express them
with people around us—
not for them to agree or validate those beliefs,
but for them to have a richer understanding
of us and our inner world.
It's important to listen to each other
with a compassionate, nonjudgmental ear.
We can disagree and have civil discussions
about our disagreements
in a respectful manner.
People will easily attack you for thinking differently from them,
even if you aren't trying to conform them into anything.
Sharing doesn't mean inflicting.
It means valuing others so much
you open your inner world for them to see.
I think it's beautiful to acknowledge this fact—
the fact that someone is opening up his heart
and being his true self around you.

104. UNRAVEL

Open your heart,
hide in the shade for a bit
with me,
and if it starts to chill,
we can look into the sun together.

105. DECEPTION

People can go on to deceive,
manipulate, and betray one another their entire lives,
but they can't fully deceive themselves.
So, when they lay in bed at night alone
with nothing but their heart and mind speaking to them—
they know.
They know even successful manipulation
isn't an accomplishment.
They know the love (or lack thereof) they give
is the love they are to receive in return.
Although it might seem like some people have no conscience,
the heart knows and the heart aches.
For we are all Love.
Being unable to love goes against our nature
and unnatural things can never ease the mind
or create happiness in one's inner world.

106. ANYWAY

Your smile will be ridiculed
by those who live in misery.
They will judge you.
Smile anyway.

Your light will blind
those who live in darkness,
even though they need it most.
Shine anyway.

Your heart will be misunderstood
by those not meant to be on your path.
Listen to its beat anyway.

Your love will be rejected
by those who are overcome with self-loathing.
Share it anyway.

107. BEFORE I GO

My smile,
my voice,
my touch,
my time.
These are the things
I'd like to share
with the world
before I go.

108. INFLUENCE ONE ANOTHER

We all constantly
influence one another—
with our words,
our actions,
and our presence.
Make it a positive influence
which echoes through eternity
and into the soul
of each person you encounter.

109. FELLOW MAN

Let us rejoice in the miracle and beauty of our fellow man.

110. FRIENDSHIP

Friendship is the greatest and most difficult possession.
It is rare and beautiful.
Friendship takes time, patience, and understanding to develop.
A friend does not judge, rather guides you through hard times.
In friendship, you love the other for who he is.
You trust the other will be there when you need him most.
And no distance or time apart can diminish such trust.

III. FRIENDSHIPS LIVED

There are many friends we lose
along the way—
a byproduct of growing apart
or maybe growing up.
And when you think about those friends,
it's best to think of them with a smile—
reminiscing of the closest moments
you shared together.
It is beautiful to know there are people
you knew so well—
people who have probably grown so much
they are new ones now.
Isn't that what life is all about?
Making bonds.
No matter how short or long-lived.
Take joy in being part of each other's lives.

112. MOURN THE LIVING

I mourn the living
with every breath.

113. SUICIDAL MAN

I wonder
how many people regretted
giving their lives away
the very last second
before the rope cut deep
into their circulation
and it was too late.
I wonder how many people
would choose a different death
if they knew what it'd be like
to surrender the last breath.
How many would choose the same?
Is it possible
this life
is to be lived and not only
forced upon us?
How can we convince
all these saddened hearts
that Love surrounds us?
What's the last memory
of a suicidal man?
A rope around the neck,
a gun or a knife at hand.
What is he leaving behind,
and why doesn't it all matter?
It doesn't take much
for the body to shatter.
We have to fight daily

to stay sane.
In your heart,
let only love remain.
Mourning the broken
echoes,
the cries into the eternal
for those who prepared
their own funeral.
So, we say goodbye
and release the hurt into the Universe.
Hoping they find salvation
in every verse.

Countless people suffer from depression and thoughts of suicide.
Lately, we have heard about many celebrities who have taken their lives.
But we only hear about them because they're in the public eye.
There are many unknown, unnamed civilians who commit suicide on a daily
basis—people who suffer silently and leave our world too soon.
This poem is dedicated to them and to all who ever felt life isn't worth living.
Fight on, my fellow beings.
Life, although difficult at times, is at its core a blessing.
Do things you love and happiness follows!

114. BORROW

Don't look into my eyes,
or you might see my sorrow.
Live on today—
there might be no tomorrow.
Time is a facade
I simply ask to borrow.
Don't look into my eyes,
or you might see my sorrow.

115. SORROW

Does sorrow show in the blink of an eye?
Beyond the laughter, can you see what's inside?
The aching pains of a heart so strong;
a wounded warrior keeps forging on.

When all seem weakened he powers through
giving light is all he knew.
"How much longer?" he yells and cries.
But a joyous face gets no replies.

For Light doesn't take, it only gives.
Thus solitude is where he lives.
And if he grieves for the fleeting of time,
his hurt is with me; it is mine.

But no one cares for a warrior heart.
It has survived this much thus far.
So, his tears flow onto deserted dirt.
No one to see them and no one to hurt.

Does sorrow show in the blink of an eye?
Does laughter disguise a broken sigh?
In the cracks, deep in the hole,
somewhere there we find our soul.

So, look inside there and you'll find—
although you see, you are blind.

For no one knows the trials of others,
so, let us be to one another
the most compassionate of mothers.

116. EMBRACING SORROW

I feel it creeping in—
the sadness which comes every now and then.
I refuse to indulge in all the addictions I have quit
so, embracing sorrow—
here I sit.

117. DISCONTENT

My broken heart feels like it's popping out of my chest,
and the unquiet mind can never find its rest.

118. BLEAK

Nowadays, everything seems bleak.
Tasteless food which touches the tongue,
consumed only out of necessity and nothing more.
It's just fuel needed to continue on
in a meaningless cycle of Samsara.
Sleepless nights spent tossing and turning around,
with a tired body and the fatigue of a restless mind.
Days of isolation and despair,
twilights and purgatories,
holding themselves still for mourning hearts.
The gloom fills the room
as swiftly as it burns the spirit.
There is no sunlight here.
Only glimpses of life lost
somewhere beyond the horizon of forgotten joy.

119. CRAZY GLUE

Understanding certain things on a deep level
places a huge responsibility on you
to be simultaneously compassionate and logical.
Knowing the fears and insecurities,
seeing the unhealed parts of others—
you develop an unconscious desire to help them
during the moments of your interactions.
Empathy is a skill you have been equipped with by God
because He trusts you to delicately handle this gift.
So, if you have a soft and compassionate heart,
you are holding on to a strength
which is also a purpose.
Remember it is equally important
to release energy which is not your own.
Your purpose is to spread Love in its purest form
and Truth is the highest form of Love.
So, continue to speak and live in Truth—
your presence, itself, can bring
Light into darkness and crazy glue to broken hearts.

120. GLUE TOGETHER

You can glue together
pieces of a broken heart
with hard work—
not by focusing on the heart
or gluing it together,
but by working hard
on something you love.

121. UNDERSTANDING MORALITY

Only by understanding morality
can we defeat the situational forces
which bring out the evil side of humanity.

122. REAL LOSS

You lose things you love
when you love things you lose.

123. END

How can you hate anyone
when you're aware of life's impermanence?
Each of us will die one day—
a truly humbling Truth.
Others may hurt you, betray you,
(unknowingly hurting themselves in the process),
but you can and should forgive—
even from a distance.
But hate is ignorance.
Don't unnecessarily hold on to
pain which has passed.
When anger poisons your heart,
remember: it's all just ripples in time.
Remind yourself of the bigger picture.
The picture which will inevitably have
three bold letters across the screen,
spelled out clearly in the closing credits.
END.

-ACKNOWLEDGMENTS-

I want to express my gratitude for everyone who made this book possible.

Thank you to my editor, Jaclyn Reuter.
Thank you to my cover designer, Danijela Mijailovic.

Thank you to my family and friends for loving and accepting me as I am.

Thank you to my parents for their amazing upbringing.

Thank you to Galatia Kitsios for being a nurturing and caring mother.

Thank you to my dear father, Ioannis Kitsios. I miss you and I love you. Thank you for being my guardian angel and protecting me. I will forever treasure our sacred and unique bond.

Thank you to my Nathaniel Ezra. Your constant expression of deep affection, desire, and love endlessly humbles me. I am eternally grateful to be loved by such a kind and spiritual man. You are a gift from God in my life.

Thank you to all living beings with whom I have the honor, privilege, and blessing of sharing existence.

Thank you to my heart for showing the way towards my life's purpose and God's will. I am grateful for each heartbeat.

Thank you to the air I breathe which sustains my life and nurtures my body.

Thank you to God for creating, protecting, loving, guiding, and encouraging me on the path. With your Love, I can survive it all. With your Love, there is nothing to fear.

I vow to remain humble, open, and kind until my last breath.

-ABOUT THE AUTHOR-

Maria Kitsios is a New York licensed massage therapist, Reiki master, and certified yoga instructor. *The Heart's Journey* is the fourth of a seven books series and is composed of poems related to the heart chakra. Her previous three books are *The Journey to Source*, *Unravel the Veil*, and *The Vessel of Truth*.

Join Maria's newsletter
and receive a free copy of the asanas guideline.

www.subscribepage.com/thejourneytosourceasanas

Instagram: @mkitsioslmt
Facebook: @Maria Kitsios, LMT

Made in the USA
Middletown, DE
04 September 2022

73181412R00146